FREEDOM CRY FROM PRISON

BY D. A. Sawyers, Sr.

VOLUME 1

ISBN: 0-75963-715-6

This book is printed on acid free paper.

1stBooks – rev. 6/14/01

TABLE OF CONTENTS

INTRODUCTION VII

AURHOR'S NOTES IX

BIOGRAPHY XI

I-WORD (FORWARD) XIII

A DEDICATION TO ALL AFRICAN WOMAN XV

ESPECIALLY TO ALL MOTHER AND MY CHILDREN'S MOTHER.................XV

YESTERDAY IS GONE 1

JAH IS ON MY SIDE 2

MY ROSE GARDEN 3

A TERRIBLE THING TO WASTE..5

NATURE..6

WHAT IS THE CAGE 7

WHAT NOT TO FIGHT FOR 8

HOW LONG 9

MISERY 10

WITHOUT CONTROVERSY 11

THE SPRING 12

IN THE WILDERNESS 13

YOUR EYES..14

WHO CARES 15

WHAT I SEE IN YOU 16

HOW PRECIOUS THOU ART 17

THE SECRET TO MY HEART 18

IT'S OVER 400 YEARS 19

FEAR NOT 20

I BELIEVE IN ME 21

THE HEROES OF MY COUNTRY 22

THE FIELD STUDY 25

THE COLOR OF SPRING 26

MY FIRST LOVE 27

SAXOPHONE FRONT 28

MY THIRD EYE 29

IN THE LION'S MOUTH 31

ZONE 32

THE SNOW TRAIN 33

IT IS DARK DOWN HERE 34

HE IS THE VINE 35

AIM HIGH 36

MAMA DON'T CRY 37

THE CALAMITIES OF YESTERDAY 38

YOU ARE THE ONE 39

THE FOUNTAIN OF LIFE 40

OUT OF YOUR CAGE 41

UNITED AND STAND 42

UNITY IS STRENGTH 43

WHY DO THEY EXALT? 44

IN THE CARIBBEAN 46

O MAMA AFRICA 47

NOT TOO STRONG 49

O MY, O MINE 51

I SHALL RISE 52

I LOVE MY DASHIKI 53

YOU ARE OF THE NILE RIVER 54

BORN AGAIN AFRICA 55

WHITE SUPREMACY IS THE ENEMY 57

TEACHER/FAMILIES V. BOYS & GIRLS 58

WHY SAY NEVER 60

JAMAICA'S CULTURAL DISH 61

A FEARWELL SONG 62

O THAT'S AN AMUSING HELL 63

SLAVE MAKERS 64

HAIKU 65

HAPPY BIRTHDAY 66

SEE THE VISION 67

CASSANDRA & CALIF 69

A SPELL 71

HIS WONDERS 72

IMAGE 73

MOTHERS 74

KILLING IS A CRIME 75

THE QUEST 76

DEDICATED TO MY LOVE 77

TO MY BROTHER RYAN 79

INTRODUCTION

This book of poems is dedicated to all the oppressed, the rejected,

Down-trodden and the underprivileged, especially, those who have

Reached the crossroads of life's challenges contemplating total submission of their individual wills.

Our ancestors have experienced in totality, the heights and depths of human degradation, exploitation, social rejection, economic deprivation, political exclusion, and they did not resist or shuffle at life's challenges. They fought to death the potential-blocks that have suppressed and kept them in subhuman bondage, to ensure we may have a free course to inherit the wealth that they have fought and sacrificed their lives for.

In this book, I am endeavoring to take you to another level of consciousness through poems.

BY David Sawyers

<u>AURHOR'S NOTES</u>

In preparing this book, I asked my self,

"Where do I start my journey?"

"I will start right here," was my answer.

"Where is my destination?" I asked myself.

"Success," I plainly replied.

I am consciously aware that I am presently at the

Bottom of the pole, but I trust in the creator to

Guide my future beyond the human perception.

I will not quit, for I shall attain my goals. I

am determined to write the passage of history that

has stigmatized the outcast, Oppressed, and the

Minorities. I am determined to fight the obstacles

that have kept us de-mobilized, de-centralized,

de-humanized and ostracized.

BIOGRAPHY

<u>David A Sawyers, Sr. forth child of nine children.</u>

Born 11/5/63 a citizen of Jamaica W.I. (Decedant of Ethiopia).

Son of Miguel Sawyers and Enid sawyers of Jamaica.

I am father to five children Dean, Tian, David Jr., Lanzo, and Tanisha.

I am presently holding an A.A. degree in Urban Studies from the University of the District of Columbia and pursuing a B.A. in Urban Studies and an associate in Economics.

I-WORD (FORWARD)

Poetry, one of history's oldest art forms, it gives social credibility to creation. Within every culture, past or present, poetry gives insight into its collective identity. Poetry is a universal language that all human beings hear, speak, and understand. Brother David Sawyers belongs to the human family. And as all humans, he loves, feels, and knows great truths and lyrically expresses them in the pages that fallow.

As a creative Ethiopian Descendant from Jamaica, David Sawyers' nature is unquestionably dynamic. He came forward from the mighty mountains and rolling hills which suggests in itself a firm commitment to the struggles for unity. This skillful brother uses the word as power to convey life's realities. He dialectically utilizes the power of words both ugly and beautiful, weak and strong. His words are convictions, commitments, truths of old-don't cry, rejoice. Herein are Ethiopian realities-confinement, chaotic experiences and dreams of mystery Babylon. Brother David, like David in the bible, best describes his observations when he chants that "it's over 400 years and we (INI) have not been broken…still striving…not begging anything…now demanding…Judah rules" (19). Like black poet Langston Hughes, his stylistic approach represents continuity and empathy. Read poetry.

Forerunners of new black poetry are of course Amiri Baraka, formerly LeRoi Jones, but there are also others whose impacts are tremendously important. Poet such as David Sawyers, a good man and scholar, humble, patient, angry at times, and always…. Exodus (Movement of Jah people). One may have heard the rhythmic lyrics of dub poets, including Mutaburuka, Sam Brown, Oku Onuora, and Ras Pidow to name a few; now read Sawyers' "The Heroes of my country" (22). He brings to life Paul Bogle and Quashi. There is myth and wit in Briar Anancy and Tacooma, Sam Sharp, Nanny, Chugghu, and Marcus Garvey. Combined is history and class, working peoples' rights, and survival in the multiracial nonracial way. These poetic words pull many forward in life. Read on, I say in a "Terrible Thing to Waste" (5). His confinement today is of no surprise when so many whisked off to prisons because of mans inhumanity to man: Caribbean phenomena of which glimpses are heard in his poetic voice…

Caribbean Basin Initiative...Caricom and heads of Caribbean judgments/politics, and their failure to fine economic answers "The Calamities of Yesterday" – a legacy of colonialism (38). Then Migration- the problems encountered by many migrants on another plantation (U.S.A.) "O That's an Amusing Hell"(63).

David is a black man of principle, undoubtedly an Ethiopian intellectual, who if given a fair and equal chance could help mankind find salvation. For his uniqueness is his answers/identity to Ethiopian's, that cannot be stopped – delayed yes! But not stopped... read on.

Takuma Umoja (ndk)

Guyana

A Dedication to all African Woman

Especially to all mother and my children's mother.

"RUTH A WOMAN OF PRINCIPLE"

Woman by nature are one of God's most unique, engaging and appealing creatures. The "Book of Proverbs" states, "who can find a virtuous woman, for her price is far above rubies?" Solomon posed this age-old question that is still being asked today. This writer believes that one need only to look in the Book of Ruth in order to find a virtuous woman. Also, this writer believes that the book of Ruth is a love story, which depicts a vivid picture of one woman's loyalty, faithfulness and integrity. These God-inspired attributes gained her both favor and honor in the sight of the Israelites.

Even though Ruth was a foreigner to the Hebrew nation, she maintained a strong sense of loyalty after the death of her husband Chidion. Ruth could have easily returned to her native land like her sister-in-law, Orpah. There in her native land, a young attractive widow would have been a prime candidate for marriage. Because of Ruth's sense of loyalty and devotion, she refuse to abandon her mother-in-law, Naomi, during a time in which she was desperately needed. In a day where the divorce rate is fifty percent, we are seeing couple abandon one another at an alarming rate. In fact, not only are we seeing spouses divorce, but children are divorcing their parents and parents children. It seems as though our "modern day" sense of loyalty has taken a ride on the information highway. Ruth was committed to the Mosaic law which concerned the marriage duties of brothers. That law is found in the "book of Deuteronomy" and states, "If brethren dwell together, and one of them die, and have no child, the wife of the dead should not married outside of the family tree unto a stranger: her husband's brother should go unto her, and take her for his wife, and perform the duty of a husband's brother unto her; unfortunately, Chilion's only brother, Mahlon preceded him in death. Consequently, there was no one in Ruth's town to fulfill the "marriage duties as brothers."

It is refreshing to find a protagonist in a story who was committed to serve her family not for what they could give her, but because she was committed to Godly principles.

Ruth was extremely faithful to her mother-in-law after the deaths of her husband, brother-in-law, and father-in-law. Naomi tried to get Ruth to return to her native land on several occasions. However, Ruth was determined to dwell with Naomi. She undoubtedly was inspired by Naomi's strong will and perseverance. When presented with the option of leaving, Ruth stated, "Wherever you go, I will go: and wherever you lodge, I will lodge; your people shall be my people, and your God my God." It is fair to surmise that Ruth went above and beyond the call of duty.

The story of Ruth gives us a wonderful example of how a woman can suffer a tremendous loss and maintain her integrity. Ruth was indeed a woman of principles. After returning to her mother-in-law's hometown of Bethlehem, Ruth was confronted with the possibility of being chosen as a mate by Boaz. Instead of going after a rich man, or a young man, Ruth chose to follow the custom of the "close relative". She lie at the feet of Boaz, and asked Boaz to "take your maidservant under your wings, for you are a close relative". In doing so, she would preserve the honor of her late husband and her late father-in-law.

In this dramatic love story, we can see how Ruth's faithfulness, loyalty and integrity gained her both favor and honor in the sight of the Hebrews. In fact, those were the exact attributes that attracted Boaz to Ruth. As Ruth lie at Boaz's feet he would tell her to "do not fear..., for all the people of my town know that you are a virtuous woman. In a day and age where we are constantly talking about a return to family values, the story of Ruth presents an interesting analogy. This story serves as a good "measuring stick" for our woman of today.

<u>Yesterday Is Gone</u>

Yesterday is gone, but my experience will help

shape my tomorrow. It was dark, gloomy, and hopeless.

But my persistence to create a better future

has never yet ceased.

Obstacles and potential blacks have given

me a hard fight, they cause my face to wrinkle,

they cause my heart to despair, but thanks be to

JAH, for I have not lost my mind.

I hope and pray, time after time that my yesterday

will help shape my tomorrow, for it will serve as

a stepping-stone, a guidepost, and a medium by

which I can pyramid to my future. Yesterday is gone,

but tomorrow is still to come.

I will fight the mental, emotional, economic, and

educational struggles, and most of all, the socialistic

struggles. Yesterday is gone, but my experience will enable

me to stand for the rights of humanity. My persistence

Will fortify my hope for a better tomorrow, which will

not be lived in vain. Yesterday is gone

what's up with tomorrow?

It depends on what I do today.

By David Sawyers

<u>JAH IS ON MY SIDE</u>

JAH is on my side, else time would have left me
no tomorrow.
JAH is on my side, that is why I can see another
hour.
In my youth, I have struggled while others played.
I have suffered hunger while others chose delicacies
I played soccer with milk cartons box while others
played with prestigious leather soccer balls.
Jah is on my side, else time would have left
me no tomorrows.
JAH is on my side, that is why I can see another
hour.
I have attended schools in ransacked barns while
others attended modern architectural design
schools.
I have settled for the back row while others
enjoyed the privilege of the front.
I have worked your fields, plowed your rows,
cut your cane, while you sent your children to college.
I will stand and fight, and I will not be an
Opportunists while my brothers suffer and die.
JAH is on my side, else I would have been long gone.

By David Sawyers

<u>MY ROSE GARDEN</u>

My rose garden was given to me by the owner
of all vineyards.
I have a special love for my rose garden because
it has become my heart's desire.
Before my vineyard would yield any vine, I would
care for it as a nursing mother cares for
her suckling.
I'd plowed it in the spring time and watered it
in the summer.
My rose garden was gorgeous and desirable.
My rose garden was so desirable that I'd planted
my first fruit tree in the winter season.
The snow came in a blistered fashion, and it
stripped all the leaves from my first plant.
The snow took all the life substance from my lovely
plant.
I wept and shed tears, but there was no hope
for my precious plant, yet my rose garden was
still desirable to me.
In the spring my rose garden cried out to me
in a special way. There was a need to replow
my garden that it might produce her choicest
fruit. So I was compelled to work.
In the fall my precious rose garden brought
forth a male tree and two summers after my first
tree, my rose garden yielded a female tree.
now I am away from my garden and I'm unable to
tend to the trees.

But they shall not perish but live.

I love my rose Garden and the trees that it bares.

By David Sawyers

<u>A terrible Thing to Waste</u>

The mind is a terrible thing to waste.

So why wait?

The opportunity is at the gate, so why

Procrastinate?

If you miss today, you may very well miss

The foundation, and without a foundation

whereon shall you build?

the mind is like an infant.

It is progressive.

If you neglect an infant it will die.

Surely, if you neglect the mind it will also

Decease.

By David Sawyers

<u>NATURE</u>

Nature is my best teacher. It shall serve as
my genuine guide.
It cools my brow and my lips with fresh water
from heaven.
Nature is a valley, its greenery is like a
plush carpet under my feet. By it the lilies
are sustained.
Nature is the sun and the moon and by their
presence lives flourish.
The rain gives forth water and it moisturizes
the earth.
Nature allows the water to intermingle with
plants and all living things both on the face of the
Earth and in the depths of the seas.
the sun serves as magnetic force which causes
the moistness to be vaporized and condensed
in order that it may reproduce more rain for
the services of creation.
likewise man shall produce and reproduce, for
mankind is nature and nature is man's creator.
Nature is my best teacher!!!

By David Sawyers

<u>What is the Cage</u>

Scientists have created the cage.

The cage is a means to restrain animals

and birds for the propose of observation and experimentation.

They observed the behavior of animals and beasts

in order to see how they commune to co-exist in

isolated environments.

Scientists have experimented on animals' reaction

to the cage.

It amused them to deprive and demobilize God's creation.

Scientists have defiled the Laws of Jah.

Scientists have created the cage.

By David Sawyers

What Not to Fight For

I will not fight for human rights because

I am one hundred percent human.

I will not fight for equality because I was created

the dominant one.

I will not fight for legalization and exploitation

of humanity for I am not proclaiming superiority.

I will not fight to persuade others that I am

above and not beneath for the pigmentation of

my skin explains it all.

I will not fight for your land because I have

my own.

I will not fight for your woman because

I am obsessed with the glowing beauty of my African

women.

I will not fight for your vineyard because it

does not produce my kind of fruit.

Live and left me alone because what you have

is worth nothing, nothing that I should fight for.

By David Sawyers

<u>How Long</u>

How long shall I wait before my equal rights
can be fully guaranteed?
How long shall I wait until justice can be served?
You told me that heaven is above and paradise is
beneath.
How long should I listen to your lies. You told
me that there is no need for me to learn now.
So I worked your fields while you send your children
to school.
They too learned to tell my children to wait.
but how long?
How long shall I be submissive?
How long will you be the aggressor?
How long can you be rich while I remain poor and
destitute for the necessities of life?
How long shall I be the pawn in your game being
subjugated and sacrificed as a pawn while you dominated
and survive having free access as kings, Queens,
Rooks, Knights, and Bishops.
How long shall I spread your red carpet that you
may parade upon me. I shall fight, especially
for the cause of humanity.
How long, not long....not anymore

By David Sawyers

<u>MISERY</u>

Misery is not my best friend, but it has stuck
closer than my desired friends.
Misery has caused me to be cognizant of my past
experience of being carefree and compassionate
towards my assumed friends.
I have given my all to my neighbors and friends.
Nevertheless, when misery takes its full effect
on my life, I was dejected, and as a man without
a history, life or future.
After all, could misery be my true teacher which
will guide me to a progressive future?
I am persuaded that my misery will lead to a
total emancipation from this unethical, demoral,
degraded, and dehumanizing, predicament that holds
me in subhuman bondage.

By David Sawyers

<u>WITHOUT CONTROVERSY</u>

Herb is a creation of Jah, and it is the healing
of the land.
Its purpose was to be consumed by man, the
beast of the field and the fowl of the air.
In the creation herb has never fail to sustain
life, if you take it away the people will weep,
the earth will wail.
Aren't you afraid that the earth will cease
to yield? Then why would you steal from humanity?
You discovered our contentment brought about by
the consumption of the holy herb. You experience
the essence of the holy herb and the exploitation
thereof, but when we attempt to survive by the
herb you enlarged you prisons and lighted
your chains against our arm, feet and neck.
Aren't you afraid now that you have discovered
that the war you fight is not man but Jah.
The herb is "sacred" and it's the healing of
the land and the sea.

By David Sawyers

<u>THE SPRING</u>

A spring sprang forth from the Carving Rocks.
It is the life support of the forests of Lebanon.
It sustained its inhabitants.
The spring gives life to everything that comes
in contact with it.
The birds of the air were extremely appreciative
of her.
The beast of the field have always rejoiced
to have her in their presence.
All of creation has greatly desired to behold its
life giving source.
The spring of Lebanon is eternally dedicated
to its inhabitants.
Can the spring of Lebanon be forgotten?

By David Sawyers

IN THE WILDERNESS

I am in the wilderness.

I have chosen the wrong paths.

It does no good to jog, run or

Increase my stride in the wilderness.

For I have taken the wrong path.

What will it cost?

I will pay for what's lost.

By David Sawyers

<u>YOUR EYES</u>

Your eyes are as a dove's eyes.
They are lovely and sensitive.
I love to behold them because they unlock the
secret treasure door to your heart and reveal
the inner parts of your souls.

The early morning sun has reflect and send
a sparkling image to your light brown eyes.
Your eyes immediately send me in an emotional
frenzy.
I am mesmerized beyond comprehension.
The spell has been cast.
Your eyes are as a dove's eyes.

By David Sawyers

<u>WHO CARES</u>

Who are you to say,

What is right from what is wrong?

are you a human?

That I can't over stand

why do you promote segregation?

Yes, you have invaded the motherland

you have exploited the first, second, and

third generation.

you reside them in your large plantation…

don't you know that your actions were immoral,

inhuman and unethical?

By David Sawyers

WHAT I SEE IN YOU

The things I see in you are things of quality.
Things that are true.
You possess the attributes of God himself…
Things that I long for.
In your eyes you hold the compassion for the
world, and in your soul, are jewels, more precious
than black pearls.
Your hands, how they caress. They soothe the
savage beast, they tell a tale. Your words are a
song. With elegance they ring. The melody of my
heart is inspired by your hymns.
The qualities you possess my sweet, are of
innocence and virtuosity.
They reflect the glow of your countenance.
When I see your face, love, honor,
All of the spiritual gifts,
The qualities of a wife are the things
I see in your life, so continue to strive, future
bride, until such a time as the master designates.
The things I see in you are things of quality.

By David Sawyers

HOW PRECIOUS THOU ART

How precious art thou? To my heart, you're more
precious than pure gold.
How precious art thou? To my eyes, you are a gem
refined from coals.
How precious art thou? Lovely, as the morning dew
you have changed my life, my world's anew.
You are the fairest among the kinds ten thousands.
There is none like you in all his kingdom.
How precious thou art? Greater than one could
Imagine. To fathom your worth one couldn't
comprehend. Your value is immeasurable, this I do
understand.
how precious thou art?

By David Sawyers

THE SECRET TO MY HEART.

The secret to my heart, you hold the key, unlock

my mind, and set me free.

It can only be done with the love that you have,

your gentle kiss is like balm and salve.

It's liken unto a puzzle and you're the missing

part, you hold my mind, my soul, my heart.

Come lay me down, sprawled upon the meadows

grass, where the lilies and Sharon roses are in full blast.

The key is within thee, no secret to be left

untold; be gentle, be strong, forever to

be bold....

By David Sawyers

<u>IT'S OVER 400 YEARS</u>

Its been over 400 years and we have not been
broken.
Its been over 400 years and wee are still striving.
Its been over 400 years and we are not begging
anything.
Its been over 400 years and we are now demanding
what is rightly ours.
Its been over 400 years and what we are demanding is
FREEDOM, JUSTICE, and EQUALITY.
Its been over 400 years and we have not been broken.

By David Sawyer

<u>FEAR NOT</u>

Fear not ye almighty race.

Fear not ye mighty people.

Thy redeemer has come.

Thy wealth has been restored.

Fear not for thou art dignified in all aspects.

Because of Jah you have respect.

Fear not, for thou hast endured the chains,

the whips, the ropes, the fires, the brands,

the ships—that brought you here from the Mother

Land.

Because of Jah we join hand in hand.

Fear not for Thy rewards shall be in full.

It shall be enough for thy children, and their

children to the fourth and fifth generations

because of Jah we maintain our integrity.

By David Sawyers

I BELIEVE IN ME

I believe in me because

apart from me there is no life I can see…

I believe in me because life I know lies

within me…

I believe in me because it is I, and Jah alone who

control my destiny.

I believe in me….

I believe in me….

By David Sawyers

THE HEROES OF MY COUNTRY

The heroes of my country, their stories

are not untold.

they may be transcended, but their spirits

are not cold.

Speaking of Quashi,

He was very bold.

In order to survive

He did what he was told.

He used repetitions of question he didn't understand

in order to trick and confound the man.

You may think that he was an Uncle Tom

oh, never in your mind would you think

he was armed.

But he tricked them with obedience and remained very calm.

Brier Anancy and his son Tacooma re-established

the courage of the great Ashanti tribe among

the slaves.

Because of them they became very brave.

Touching Paul Bogle:

A spiritual leader, but human exploitation he

could not stand.

He saw the social and economic condition of

his society and he knew that they were wrong.

So he risked being killed, beaten or harmed.

He was summoned to court to face his prey

He led a coalition to Morant Bay.

In order that slaves be paid and freed.

Credit Paul Bogle for this good deed.

His men attached and wasted the Baron away.

The Baron's associates were roasted for fire

was on the way.

Oh, fateful was that day in Morant Bay.

Plantations were de-escalated by fire

Planters were killed

Uncle Tom was murdered.

could this action be plotted by one man?

They asked.

I said no; it was harmony of humanity and that's

why Paul Bogle was hung....

on a British ship called HMS Wolverine.

Sam Sharp was among the slaves in

Mo-Bay slave trade.

He rebelled against slave-traders and was

hung in Mo-Bay square.

and that's why to this day it is called

Sam Sharp Square.

Nanny was a woman, brave, powerful and strong.

Everything that the planters did - she knew they

were wrong, so she stood up as a human

tall and strong because she knew that victory would be won.

She lived in a castle with secret passages so

she could access and deliver secret messages

countless times they pursued her with death on

their minds.

But in a twinkling of an eye, she was nowhere

to be found.

They shot her and killed her, but her memories

and courage are not left untold.

Chugghu, a slave of old

but his contribution to liberation
we could never with hold.
Marcus Garvey was a patriotic man because as
A young man, he acquired education. He saw
the system in action and to his interpretation,
It was immoral, so in news-form, he published it
to everyone. He hipped the people to repatriation.
That didn't suite the Caucasian because their
Workers were learning about their born land for
in reality they were true Africans.
He traveled the seventh seas and the Caribbean,
he spoke against human exploitation.
They created his sickness and demobilized the
movements but his prophesy of redemption was
carried on.

By David Sawyers

THE FIELD STUDY

My Field study has taken me from my born land

to the land of the rich and affluent.

I was in search of the golden hen and her

geese's which laid the golden eggs. I have

learned that with wealth I cannot be refuted.

Not that its wealth was the ultimate, but its fame

has escalated to the height of its peak. This is

why my field study has brought me to this land.

My field study has revealed that for the rich

there is much more to be given them than the poor.

For the poor, there is neither a plate nor a home. Ice cream

they eat, but not from a cone. Mothers weep and

Fathers morn because their first night's meal they

have none. They work for a living but in reality

it was just a killing because their employers would

not offer them a skill for their healing. How can

they be still after taken that pill. Can't they see

that it's a spell. It was conceived, designed

and plotted well.

My field study shows that in this system the

rich must go in order that the poor may know

that they too play a major role in this economic

show. Then they will ask this question: isn't

this something we should have known?

By David Sawyers

<u>THE COLOR OF SPRING</u>

The colors of spring have a spectrum
of life-giving, energizing, and regeneration
spirit that gives life to mysteries untold.
The colors of spring are not as winter, gloomy and
gray. The colors contain all the colors within a
wide spectrum. They are life giving, magnificent,
and brilliant.
The colors of spring have remained a constant
magnetic force. They attract all classes of insect,
the beast of the field and the fowl of the air.
I am in awe of the colors of spring.

By David Sawyers

<u>MY FIRST LOVE</u>

My first love was the one that I thought was for
me. Beyond her beauty I could not see. She was
beautiful, young, fresh and pure. I had found
her very attractive and desirable to be had.
Her eyes were as dove's eyes. Her teeth were
white as ivory and had a sparkling shine that reflects
the innocence of her youth. Her face was the
complexion of burnt brass untouched. She was
pure. Her eyebrows were thick and black as eve.
Her hair was black, curly and shiny. She had
Childish plats revealing her clean scalp. She
has nice long legs and clean skin. Her
appearance would have blown any man's mind
because in reality she was "fine", and all mine.
It was in the month of June, in the rising of the
Caribbean sun. the breeze was blowing creating
chills through our veins as we walk along the sea
shores of Walter Fletcher beach. She wore an
extra large thin white cotton T-shirt and short
wrangler corduroy pants. The sun was descending
beneath our feet. I held her hands she held mine
as we walked along the beach and talked.

By David Sawyers

SAXOPHONE FRONT

There is a song of love in my heart.

It's set aflame by your eloquence of word.

Ah, that's the spark.

The music I will play on this instrument of

grace. Oh, how long to serenade you face to

face.

Come join me in my sweet, symphonic poem

of life.

Where god is the composer and we are his splendid

work of art.

There is a song of love in my heart.

By David Sawyers

MY THIRD EYE

My third eye is not shy. It is crowded
with cherubim from beyond the skies. It
doesn't see what is dedicated to it.
My third eye sees the horizons and far
beyond. It permeates the horizontal as
well as the vertical.
You may ask why a third eye but to you I
will say, "why not?"
My third eye can jaunt beyond my natural
vision. Why should I rely on the natural
alone when I am more than natural. My
natural eyes only see the obstacles which
are present. My third eye sees the things that
are oblivious to my natural eyes. My natural
eyes see its surrounding very clearly but my
third eye has a definitive vision of the
will of my provider.
You may ask why a third eye but to you I
will say, "why not?"
You may ask why, how, when, and where
does a man attain unto wisdom, knowledge
and over standing. But if you consider the
third eye you'll know why.
My natural eyes can see the tunnel but
the third eye sees the light at the end
of the tunnel. My third eye is the only
eye that helps to shape and narrow out
the pathway of life.

You may ask why a third eye but to you I
Will say "why not?"

30

By David Sawyers

IN THE LION'S MOUTH

Your hands are in the lion's mouth.

So why did you squabble about your

hands in the lion's mouth.

Be quiet and don't shout your doggish mouth.

He was hungry and looking for something

to swallow and that's when you came

about began to holler.

He then discovered a meal and started to growl,

but in stead you humble, you started to holler.

Your hands are in the lion's mouth, so be

articulate and take them out.

It is not too late to take a round about

in stead you want to be stupid and shout.

By David Sawyers

<u>ZONE</u>

I was traveling alone a strait path.

Along the way, I notice an attachment of zones.

Zones to walk.

Zones to talk.

Zones to laugh

Zones to eat

and zoon to sleep

in the sleeping zone, I decided to talk so I had

to retract,

because everything that was asleep had started

to walk toward me with knives and forks.

In the eating zone, I decided to walk but I had

no spark because everyone seems as though they

had seen a shark.

In the laughing zone, I decided to talk but back

off. I had to walk for the people would hit me all-sorts of ways.

Into the eating zone, I decided to sleep, but in their

mind they thought I was cheap,

so they hit me with all sorts of chide.

In the walking zone I decided to sleep, but look out, they were stepping on me

with their feet.

So now I have become a zone freak.

I will stay in my zone.

better find your zone ... own your own

By David Sawyers

<u>THE SNOW TRAIN</u>

I have taken the snow train and my destination

Was anywhere and everywhere.

The ride was smooth, but it leads to fear.

A part of it, I didn't want to share.

Ah, the spell it cast on me. I didn't want to care.

The door was knocking, and I began to

fear. I rushed to the window and didn't

stop to peer. I had refused to sit even

though I had a chair. Ah, the spell it

cast on me.

My wife was gone and my children would be crying.

The snow train was escalating, so I just stood

There shaking.

Ah, the spell it cast on me.

By David Sawyers

<u>IT IS DARK DOWN HERE</u>

It is dark down here, and it's getting
even darker.
It's dark down here and it's not getting
any better.
It is dark down here because it was
planned to be this way.
It is dark down here because up on our
Race they have preyed

By David Sawyers

HE IS THE VINE

He is the vine and we are the branches.

He is the vine and we possess the fruit

of his labor.

He is the vine, and he gives authority

to the branches to posses those

qualities in which he so desires..

he is the vine, and what he has

predestined can by no means be tainted

but must prosper.

By David Sawyers

<u>AIM HIGH</u>

As high as the heavens are above the
Earth, so are my aims beyond the human
perceptions.
As high as the highest mountain above
the valleys, higher are my objectives in
this life and the one to come.
As high as I reach, so high and higher I
will achieve.

By David Sawyers

MAMA DON'T CRY

Mama don't cry

Mama don't cry

You did labored

and were rewarded

with princes' and princess'

mama don't cry

mama don't cry

you have been blessed

and was rewarded with rich soil

and fresh streams.

Mother don't cry because you were

blessed with sons and daughters to help

keep you a shining light.

Mother don't cry

Mother don't cry

because your reward is on his way

home.

By David Sawyers

<u>THE CALAMITIES OF YESTERDAY</u>

The misfortunes of yesterday have poisoned our minds,
it has paralyzed our motivation and demobilized our sense
of purpose.
The catastrophes of yesterday have disarmed and
set us back a few hundred years.
The mishaps of yesterday were a stumbling block in
which we shall turn into a stepping-stone for future growth.

By David Sawyers

<u>YOU ARE THE ONE</u>

You are the cream of my life,

so why does my coffee remain black

You are a desirable flavor,

So why do my taste buds remain unpleasant.

You are the scarecrow that keeps

the wild beast from attacking me,

So where were you when I was being

invaded by the undesirable.

You are the bee that produces my riches

and favorable honey.

Without you in my life, I have no desirable

sweetness to satisfy my life.

By David Sawyers

<u>THE FOUNTAIN OF LIFE</u>

There is a fountain of life that is
flowing out of me, and it is unstoppable.
There is a fountain of life that is
flowing out of me. It is good for the
rich as well as the poor.
There is a fountain of life that is
flowing out of me and if you listen and
take heed, you will live and not die.
There is a fountain of life that is
flowing out of me. That is God's divine
and inspiring words of deliverance and
life eternally, come take a drink!

By David Sawyers

<u>OUT OF YOUR CAGE</u>

Come- - out of your cage that has

suppressed you for so long and be

welcome into my castle of rubies

diamonds, and pearls.

days have passed

weeks have passed

months have passed

…and now years have passed

jump into the millennia strive.

hurry - - out of your cage that has

suppressed you for so very long and be

welcome into my castle of rubies,

diamonds, and pearls. Jump into the millennia strive.

It makes me weep to see you trapped in

your cage.

Daily I have passed you by. I can see

your anger and frustrations. You tend

to hold it back, but you undoubtedly find that it

is hard to suppress. However, the day

will come when you'll notice that your

cage is in fact wide open. Then you'll

be free to invade my castle of rubies,

diamonds and pearls, by jumping into the 21st century

millennia strive.

It makes me weep to see you trapped in

Your cage.

By David Sawyers

<u>UNITED AND STAND</u>

United we stand -on one accord.
Divided we fall - - scattered, unstabled
and abroad.
United we can conquer all…
possess our wealth wherein we dwell…
redeem our soul from the untimely hell.
organize and centralize, keep our
society alive. We are the nation that
will not take any bribes.
keep your spirit alive for we are like
the bees in the beehives.
United we stand,
…but divided we will fall.

By David Sawyers

UNITY IS STRENGTH

Working in your corn field masa, you

it appeals,

burning sun, my skin it peels.

I am thirsty, but your whip I can feel.

Oh, mother Africa would you once again

re-appear?

Cutting your bananas stacking them in

boxes. Oh, snakes were vicious on the

Attacking. I became your human fork-lift

stacking bananas in a ship.

And still your wicked heart did not

spare me from the whip.

Oh, mother Africa would you once again

re-appear?

The coconut trees were tall, but on them

You commanded me, you say "boy don't fall'

"Yes masa" was my all. Even though I

know I could.

By David Sawyers

<u>WHY DO THEY EXALT?</u>

Why doeth the strong pray on the weak? and why do they
rest while the weak stay on their feet? Is it because they
assumed the weak are strong and those that are posed
as the strong are in reality the weak?

> Why doeth the least exalted ones exalt themselves?
> It is because they are afraid to expose themselves
> and become depressed, oppressed, rejected, and
> finally the unethical bastards as they
> really are.

They have invaded mount Zion, from whence came the
black man. Our ancestors were tricked, kidnapped, and
raped, sold to slave masters, beaten at the stake. Posing
themselves as missionaries, we open our world to them.
Friendly they came and friendly we received them, but their
hearts were subtle as serpents and viciously wicked.
With chains they took our sons, and with cords they binded
our daughters, and they auctioned them off to the slave masters.

> Our foreparents were taken from the
> shores of Africa in ships as human
> cargoes. On their way to Europe, Spain, France,
> America, and the Caribbean.
> Some were thrown to the belly of the
> oceans, from were no man would return.
> These actions I still can't understand.
> Could these wicked and unethical acts
> proceed from any man.

Now, in sincerity, the oppressors are the incomplete
man. That is why their exalted actions must come to an

end. They will know that they were not made to rule over the original men (Black men).

45

By David Sawyers

<u>IN THE CARIBBEAN</u>

In the Caribbean, early in the
morning prior to the rising of the
sun, the birds sung their songs
releasing sounds mesmerizing to the
hearing and harmonizing in the
presence of JAH'S creations.
Putting the whole island under
observation. They were peering in
unification.
Oh, it was a sensation and
gratification rising up in the Caribbean.

By David Sawyers

O MAMA AFRICA

O Mama Africa…

O Mama Africa…

You are not a tribe

nor an island

or a country,

so why are your inhabitants in exile?

Why have you been conquered?

…when you are a continent with men of valor.

Egypt is your oldest daughter,

from her flows a fountain of knowledge.

The whole world acquires her unsearchable

Inventions, and innovations, she is the keeper

of the hidden mysteries of Isis and Horus.

She was kind in her giving, but her kindness

Has become unto her a partial destruction.

O Mama Africa…

O Mama Africa…

You are a fortified nation.

From whence cometh the African men.

Rise and help us stand.

Irrefutable, we are strong.

We have endured the attacks of annihilation.

for in us our creators have ingrained their

plans.

so yes Mama Africa, you are the ultimate one,
The original land from whence came the
black men.

By David Sawyers

NOT TOO STRONG

I hope that I am not coming on too strong.

Because I have seen a true Nubian.

Could it be a dream or a vision?

When I first saw you, you were under

total observation.

for me to with hold my true emotion,

I would be less than a human,

so please try to understand that I am

Not coming on too strong.

In reality, could I be wrong/

If not, be my woman because I am an

original man, and that is all you should

understand without any contemplation.

My eyes have seen you,

I was hypnotized

You were mesmerized,

Can I be your future prize?

Be my queen and accept this crown of mine's.

be welcome to sit by my throne,

And my heart, it you can own.

If I am wrong,

just let me understand,

for my eyes have seen a true Nubian.

I am young, and you are fresh and green,

so it must be a vision that put us in Union,

and that's what made us a combination.

You are a strong Nubian.

For you came from the original man.

By David Sawyers

<u>O MY, O MINE</u>

In a twinkling of on eye I shall venture far beyond

the skies.

My work will be over and my heart will be crying

O My, O Mine…

My voice I will not suppress

My sprit is at its best.

My words are hitting,

and people are repenting.

My heart is crying

O My, O Mine…

My work will be over when to humanity

it is offered.

Then my heart will be crying

O My, O Mine…

In a twinkling of an eye

Victory shall be mine

My heart will no longer cry,

But to the wicked, I will say…

Bye—Bye.

for my rewards shall be mine, and only mine

By David Sawyers

I SHALL RISE

I am down in the valley,

But on top of that endless

mountain I shall place my feet again.

In the valley I am walking,

there is no place to rest my tired feet.

Time after time my palms are on my cheeks.

"I am tired," I cried, and my feet are weak.

I was not hired to work -

as one that was doing a job,

so in my spirit I refuse to get mad.

Oh, isn't that sad?

Freedom mentally,

spiritually

and physically

shall make me glad..

By David Sawyers

<u>I LOVE MY DASHIKI</u>

I love my dashiki

because it is not freaky.

It is big, roomy, and it conceals me.

It is not immoral,

but it is cultural.

My dashiki is colorful, bright,

and not skin tight,

so when I ware it, I do not itch,

and my skin does not bite,

if you see my dashiki in sight,

you may say that's all right,

for dashiki dressing is black man's

pride.

By David Sawyers

<u>YOU ARE OF THE NILE RIVER</u>

You are the garden of the Nile River
and your fruits are precious and of a
tender touch.
You are better to me than ten virgins
Because your garden has never went dry.
Your breasts to me are like ten cushions
that give comfort to a lover untouched.
you are bold, and my love, you will
never grow old. When I am in your arms
and they are fold around me, chill bumps
rise in me like winter, yet I am not cold.
You are the garden of the Nile River.
Come and quench my thirst before the
Spring in me burst. You are my number one
and with you I need not a second hand.

By David Sawyers

BORN AGAIN AFRICA

I am a new born African, for I have been born again

Into a new state of consciousness of my original predecessors.

I was brain washed, color splashed – with white wash—covering

that which was black—-trying to hide the true rack of age –with genetic attacks

upon all that is born black. Conscientiously aware of the original

African as the incubator…who transmitted and gave birth to the albinos—Winos

you know…we rejected you …Out cast…Bread fast, remembering

your past and want us to get lost because of your trifling past.

Psychologically you are the inferior…To the superior—become a traitor

to your original African father and mother the yellow, brown, red, and

white maker. You attacked us with the…GUN-GENOCIDE: CRACK-HOMICIDE:

HEROIN-KILL BRAIN SIZE: CIGARETTE-CANCER IN DISGUISED…

MARIJUANA—-political dive—- spraying chemical like herbicide…

annihilating the cogitating element on the mind.

PRISON HOUSE —- in retrospective is a reconstruction

Of the plantations warehousing human—- you and I as barbarians.

Academic—Behavioral bribe teaching a systematical

<u>Euro-centric view creating regression</u> resulting to a

mental genocide.

ECONOMIC—- HUNGRY TIDE—-socially-hurting our

pride—-killing out the aboriginal man <u>through starvation</u>

and <u>depletion of the soul</u>. <u>AID EPIDEMIC</u>——Back firing sky high…

destroying the designer, HIS SEEDS, and no doubt, his targets

alike…. I am a new born African, for I have been born again into a new state of consciousness.

"How can he be born again when he is old?" you asked.

Well, I am conscientiously aware of the genetic inferiority of the ruling class

which psychologically put the Africans at the bottom of every race.

You said that I have no race, but I come to tell you to your face that

African is the original incubator that transmitted and gave birth to the

albinos…winos…you know,

Who in turn gave birth to you.

By David Sawyers

<u>WHITE SUPREMACY IS THE ENEMY</u>

White Supremacy is the enemy of many millions
white, red, yellow, and black, men, women, and
children.
Invaded the lands of the Indians, Iranians, Irishmen, Iraqis,
Mexicans, Columbians, Palestinians, and the Mother land.
Rape the women and murder the men just to accomplish
your devious plans.
Classifying others as barbarians, it is assuming the beginning
of civilization. Dealing in corruptions, it is polluting
the land with wars, bombs, and nuclear weapons.
Radiating and activating poisonous chemicals upon other humans.
Disregarding God's creation, it is assuming the number one
possession in world domination. Apartheid is being practice
worldwide in disguised disputing the inequalities of men,
they are instituting segregation. Arguing the superiority of
monarchy, they attained two party. The Democratic was
to brainwashed and confused the people, and the Republican
was to "con," oppressed, suppressed, depressed and keep
the people in subhuman bondage. But with God's help,
through education, and organization, we shall learn the
Method to defeat. The white superman (white
Supremacy) and his diabolic plans.

By David Sawyers

TEACHER/FAMILIES V. BOYS & GIRLS

How can the families become so complacent when

their sons and daughters are in the streets being wasted.

Yes, the system is attacking.

We know that it's not working. The virus is spreading

people are dying; children lack understanding, and are

falling victims to the killings. Babies are crying.

Mothers stop caring. The whole world is in an upheaval,

For the epidemic is spreading.

How comes the teachers become unfamiliar with children's

behavior. They are despising one for another working with

the sisters, they forget the importance of the brothers

brining up on themselves swift destruction.

The prison houses and the morgues,

They put in action, for brothers killing one another by the

faction.

families be not relax,

For your sons, and daughters are on the

attack.

Teachers, get in your rightful minds,

and teach black boys how to be men and

rulers of this land.

Families, teachers, and children are

Interrelated.

And together we can nullify the

destructive plots of the attacker, and

with jubilance our children shall have won.

By David Sawyers

<u>WHY SAY NEVER</u>

Why say never, when this life on earth

is not forever?

You are black, beautiful and clever.

Can't you see that your ability can mount you up the

ladder.

Why believe a lie, and are ready to die.

Your mother said that you would not

amount to…

your friends have told you that you are good for ….

Your teachers said that your light is going out…

you shouted at her …

turned about and now you get kick out.

Is that what life is all about?

Is that the way to go all out?

By David Sawyers

JAMAICA'S CULTURAL DISH

Jamaica's cultural disk is Ackee and Codfish.

The ackee is grown on trees, and the codfish

is from the depth of the seas.

The ackee is yellow like gold, and it is

Good to the soul.

Its seeds are black,

excluded that from the pot, because the

earth is awaiting to reproduce that.

just make a wish…and you may end

up with Jamaica's Cultural dish…
Which is ackee and Codfish.

By David Sawyers

A FEARWELL SONG

You have a 'home' in African's land that

outshine, the sun, moon, and stars,

Its glory is far,

So on your knees

You need not to crawl.

Don't shed a tear.

only say farewell.

The soul is resting.

It beats living on earthly hell.

The birds are singing.

Wolves are howling.

The earth is accepting

The spirit is elevating,

so please stop crying and

wave your hands…

farewell,

for in Africa's land you belong.

By David Sawyers

<u>O THAT'S AN AMUSING HELL</u>

O Prison, O Prison

Am I not your maker?

Can I not shape, form

And make you?

Birds are flowing, Men

pursue and catch them,

as no desire to eat them.

so in cage they want to keep them.

O that's an amusing hell!

The beasts of the field are searching for

meals to feed their sucklings.

Men in the woods assault and catch them.

In zoos they exploit and isolate them

O what an amusing hell!!

By David Sawyers

<u>SLAVE MAKERS</u>

The methodology

that emerges the theory

which puts human beings in class category

is the ideology of

bigots, and pirates

which lead them to..

became philosophers-

they manipulate the intelligence of

others in order to impose their

theoretical view points upon them.

Having not love or regards for others,

They became bloodsuckers, animal

Lovers, vampires,

And haters of the black brothers.

By David Sawyers

<u>HAIKU</u>

(1)

yea, drums were sounding.

The ashantis were calling

Mother earth, bring forth.

(2)

horseman was chanting

thunder, thunder lets make war

for black eagle is gone.

By David Sawyers

<u>HAPPY BIRTHDAY</u>

Your birthday is always special,

Especially to me…

On your great day,

You always express nothing but quality,

For quality is you.

Isn't that true about you?

You have never been sad or blue;

My heart is here to comfort you…

HAPPY BIRTHDAY TO YOU!!!

By David Sawyers

SEE THE VISION

We may not "see" on one accord now,

but in due season, you will understand

that God the father and the son are one.

Take a look at the sun, the moon, and

the stars, can't you see that they are in perfect

unison and on one accord. Well this is

the organization and manifestation of

the father and the son's words put to action.

From creation he gave life to man.

Man defiles his laws and voluntarily

Brake his fusion creates upon himself

Dis-union, confusion, and is heading for

total destruction. The father came back in the

spirit of redemption manifesting himself in

flesh to man, but the heart of man could not

perceive, conceive, or receive the holy

one of creations. To the single sighted (natural) man, the

mystery told is confusion, but to the man of

visions (spiritual), it is the supernatural workings

of the efficient one. it seems like something little,

but God manifests himself as a baby in a cradle,

but is reasons were to heal and save you.

Furthermore, the glory of the living god is inconceivable.

It heals the blind, deaf, dumb, and the cripple.

Mau, Mau, you are the original Maroons,

The true Diaspora from Africa to the

Western shores, God the Father and the Son are one. Take a look at

the sun, the moon and the stars, can't you see that they are in perfect union and on one accord.

well this is the organization and

manifestation of the father and son's

words put to action.

By David Sawyers

<u>CASSANDRA & CALIF</u>

Calif: "come to me Cassandra.

       I am your sugar and spice..."

Cassandra: "It is dark and I can not see,

       But your voice tells a million

         stories

         Is it because I am lonely and is

         separated from my one and only?"

Calif: "it is somber in here, but my heart

         kindled,

         my stories are in millions because you

         are my number one: separated, we are

         not one, so in matrimony, we shall be in

         union.'

Cassandra: "isn't this too much for one human?

         Your words are thrilling, and my

         emotions are escalating beyond my

         comprehension."

Calif: "Well, I assess that the reaction is

         natural, for it is reality for humanity

         to exalt beyond and above its capacity

         in emotion, and be emerge in the

         neutrality of nature. Because nature

         calls unto nature to bring into

         existence that which is,"

Cassandra: "Calif, I am overly absorbed by your

         Sanity. You have captured me with

         words of charms. You have placed me in total

         ecstasy. You are clever and

brave, and in my darkness you take
away my fears

Calif: My darling, my dear, please be still and
be not afraid.

Cassandra: I am standing, but my feet are
giving. Could you give me a chair
that I can sit in?

Calif: Cassandra, unfortunately, I do not have a
Chair. You can rest in my arms and I will
Wipe away your tears.

Cassandra: sugar pie, I cannot see you, but I
Can feel your closeness.

Calif: It is you, my dear. We are, no doubt, here
as one in a pair.

By David Sawyers

<u>A SPELL</u>

The imagination of Jezebel has cast a spell, created

hell, and swelled where men shall

dwell. Men will tell…

Well, and cause others to

fell into

hell (Captive) being checked out

well…, men are placed in a cell.

They refused but are compelled.

need a lawyer, but nothing couldn't

sell because they were afraid of the

place in which to Mell, for truly,

it was a natural hell.

Jezebel has cast a

Spell, created hell, and caused it to

swell were men shall dwell.

By David Sawyers

HIS WONDERS

Day after day
Father, your wonders I see
Mankind you have created and their
actions in pure misery.
Freedom you have given
With life, it is liberating
but injustice and inequality are
prevailing their destiny.
Man to man are showing no sympathy
for human extinguishing is in super
plotting.
working the mental plantation,
invisible chains are putting man in
total rebellion.
triggering off a revolution upon the
political, economic, and social structure.

By David Sawyers

IMAGE

The image of my surroundings is that of

machoism, insecurity, uncertainty, fear

and the fearless at its best.

One has no problem puffing up his chest

whether he is from the south, east,

north, or west. Fear to lie,

yet fear to die. Laying on

his bed, he is afraid to close his eyes to sleep,

because life in this hellhole is grief.

the young men are acting old

in order to gain control of the fold,

and the old men are acting young,

in order to be in the in crowd.

the image…it is a carbon copy

The image…how can I accept it?

the image…the image….I have discovered

It, for I am the true image created in

This image of the original image

The image…

The image…

By David Sawyers

D. A. Sawyers, Sr.

<u>MOTHERS</u>

Mothers are weeping

For the lands of Africa

are being invaded.

The male children are being

taken into captivity unaware of the attack,

they couldn't fight back

only to find themselves in chains…

as cargoes…,

… on their way to a land that says

Africans are sub-human barbarians,

3/5 of a man from an uncivilized land,

but mama, you are strong and

we are your off spring…mother don't cry

for the land of Africa is still unique, sweet

where people have desires to rest the sole of their feet.

By David Sawyers

KILLING IS A CRIME

All these killings,

I say it is a crime.

I say black people, don't you lose your minds,

the crack, the coke,

the dope, and the guns,

when you posses them you think its fun time

you see Marline and you think she is fine

Angela comes and you say, she is mine,

but when you drink the wine

you think its crime time.

All these killings I say it is a crime.

I say black people, you are one of a kind

the shootings, the stabbings…

…Crippling spines.

Men are raping, killing, has nothing on their minds,

de-populating the earth drawing closer the time,

that is why I say, killing is a crime.

By David Sawyers

THE QUEST

The glorious lifestyle of the past is
a constant memory of the vision I
foresee for the future. The itinerary
is to undertake and accomplish such
pristine inherent vision,
my soul is in a constant quest to see
the manifestation of the originality of
that which was; the Community..
The family…the respect…
The love… and the caring….
My quest is giving birth, for the untold
in revealing. The mysterious puzzle is
attaching, because the soul in yearning
for its resting place.
Life is a circle…not to ride in a circus.
It goes in circle…like…giving…and
taking, living and letting others live.
war…and peace, winning….and losing..
but what you chose in this life
will determine your ending. With a lover, or
a friend, your heart can be mend, but
the quest can take you to a never
Ending journey, for life will manifest its
healing.
THE QUEST…THE QUEST…

By David Sawyers

<u>DEDICATED TO MY LOVE</u>

My love, to you I pledge my today,

for you are as bright as the sun

yesterday that gave birth to an

untold mystery, splendid, brilliant, and arrayed.

If I attempt to say… my words won't give

Way…words blockage, tongue lockage, Shyness birth,

False image displays. But in my heart, your

attractiveness it wants to obey when my emotions

takes the lead way…Suppression, Regression, and

Oppression…, is in the way,

and when I attempt to see today

my yesterday is constantly in my way.

My love my focus is on you to stay

because whole heartedly, on you my mind stays.

The visions of your eyes are as harmless as a dove's eyes.

They are sparkling and they bring chills that activate

and cause a pulsation in my blood flows.

I am mesmerize by your presence, and your almond brown

Complexion is my desirable flavor.

My love, you are liken unto a peril from Ethiopia from

whence came the original Madonna, and like the river

Nile that flows from the heart of Mount Zion. You give

life to the lilies of the shores, and my heart is in

constant quest for more.

Baby, our today can bring into manifestation our

Visions of yesterday, for to you my heart is willing saying…YEAH

YEAH…

…YEAH

By David Sawyers

If you have ever lost a love one to violence this is for you. I lost my brother to the violence of our society. Read <u>A FAREWELL SONG</u>, it will not bring your love one back, nor will it stop your heart from weeping, but it will give you a little comfort, and relieve, just as this letter will let you see that you are not alone.

TO MY BROTHER RYAN

My baby brother Ryan, with your permission, I will attempt to express my deepest sympathy and concerns of your sudden departure. It is not an easy experience, and neither is it easy for me to express the hurt, agony, and pain that I am presently experiencing due to the unethical method of execution that was inflicted upon you.

However, I want you to know that you were more than a brother or a friend. You were a peoples, person. You were the very blood that flows in my vain. And my heart is enlarged by means of my affliction because my younger brother is no more in the physical. I am wounded to my very soul, but my Emotions, I am keeping under control. The songwriter said, "If it was an enemy, then I would have known, but it was my very acquaintance whom I Walk, Labor, Dance and Merry with daily." He further states that "weeping may endure for a night, but Joy cometh in the morning."

I know that the family is weeping and the lament can be heard throughout Jamaica and the United States of America, but as God said, "vengeance is mine, and I shall surely repay!!! So to God be the glory; in addition, God's word says "All things works together for the good to them that love him, to those whom are called according to his purpose." I will not forget the special moments that we shared together because they are unforgettable. You were the best brother that a person would ever want to have.

You were caring, loving, ambitious and have a good demeanor. You have helped so many people; you have brought joy to so many hearts, life to so many lives, and insight to so many people's future. So live on my brother, for life doesn't stop here for you, it just began. So with that note I will say, so long

> My heart
>
> My friend
>
> My brother

For we shall meet again.

One love, unspeakable cannot be broken...

> Farewell...
>
> Farewell...

Ryan, you have a home in glory land that outshines the sun, moon, and stars. Its glory is far, so brother, on your knees you need not to crawl. We will not shed many tears, only to lift our hands and wave farewell...farewell. Your soul is resting; it beats living on an earthly hell. The birds are singing, wolves are howling. The earth is accepting for the spirit is elevating. So we will stop our crying and wave our hands.

    FAREWELL...

    FAREWELL...

WITH ALL MY LOVE

David Sawyers

About the Author

David A Sawyers, Sr. is the fourth child of nine children. He was born 11/5/63 as a citizen of Jamaica W.I. and a descendent of Ethiopia, the Son of Miguel Sawyers and Enid Sawyers of Jamaica. David is the father to five children: Dean, Tian, David Jr., Lanzo, and Tanisha. He presently holds an A.A. degree in Urban Studies from the University of the District of Columbia and is pursuing a B.A. in Urban Studies and an Associate Degree in Economics.